PLAN A HA

HAPPY
RIGHT
NOW

DISCOVER HOW TO ACHIEVE A LIFE OF JOY AND WONDER THAT AWAITS YOU

ALLEN WRIGHT

Table of Contents

PART 1

Chapter 1:

The Goal Is Not The Point

If you ever want to achieve your goals, stop thinking about them. I know this goes against everything anyone has ever said about achieving your goals.

Everyone says that think about one thing and then stick to it. Devote yourself to that one single goal as you are committed to your next breath. Check on your goals over and over again to see if you are still on track or not and you will get there sooner than you think.

What I am proposing is against all the theories that exist behind achieving your goals but wait a minute and listen to me.

The reason behind this opposing theory is that we spend more time concentrating on thinking and panning about our goals. Rather than actually doing something to achieve them.

We think about getting into college. Getting a Bachelor's degree and then getting our Master's degree and so on. So that we can finally decide to appear for an interview that we have dreamed about or to start a business that we are crazy about.

But these are not the requirements for any of them to happen. You can get a degree in whatever discipline you want or not, and can still opt for business. As far as job interviews are concerned, they are not looking for the most educated person for that post. But the most talented and experienced person that suits the role on hand.

So we purposefully spend our life doing things that carry the least importance in actual to that goal.

What we should be doing is to get started with the simplest things and pile upon them as soon as possible. Because life is too short to keep thinking.

Thinking is the easiest way out of our miseries. Staying idol and fantasizing about things coming to reality is the lamest thing to do when you can actually go out and start discovering the opportunities that lie ahead of you.

Your goals are things that are out of your control. You might get them, you might not. But the actions, motivation, and the effort you put behind your goal make the goal a small thing when you actually grab it. Because then you look back and you feel proud of yourself for what you have achieved throughout the journey.

At the end of that journey, you feel happier and content with what you gained within yourself irrespective of the goal. Because you made yourself realize your true potential and your true purpose as an active human being.

Find purpose in the journey for you can't know for sure about what lies ahead. But what you do know is that you can do what you want to do to your own limits. When you come to realize your true potential, the original goal seems to fade away in the background. Because then your effort starts to appear in the foreground.

A goal isn't always meant to be achieved as it might not be good for you in the end or in some other circumstances. But the efforts behind these goals serve as something to look back on and be amazed at.

Chapter 2:

Why Having Lesser Things Actually Makes You Happier

How many of you feel like spending money to acquire more stuff would make you happier because you believe having more things would bring you happiness and life satisfaction?

Now I'm not talking about basic necessities such as food, toiletries, or household appliances that you would actually use on a daily basis for the betterment of your own lives.

I'm talking about a constant need to purchase things as you go shopping at a mall, such as clothes, jackets, ornaments, cups, gadgets, bags, shoes, watches. Or even random stuff that you won't really use or need as you go on various shopping platforms online, especially during huge sale days like black friday or some other major holiday where discounts are abundant and you believe that if you don't buy this now that you are missing out on a great deal.

You might not notice this at the start, but before you know it, your house is starting to feel cluttered as every inch of your house is filled stuff with no place to put them. You might even start going to IKEA to buy shelves and cupboards to house these items in places where you will probably never see or touch them again in the foreseeable future. And they end up hidden there collecting dust.

Not to mention that all these incessant buying has also costed you money over the years.

What was once a clean home with a nice living space has turned into a cramped box of unwanted items that don't bring benefit or betterment to your lives.

How many of you can relate to that? Because that is what I used to do.

Just a few years back, when i wanted to buy clothes i would literally ransack the whole discount section of a particular store and checkout 10s of clothes in one shopping trip. And before i knew it my wardrobe was filled with so many clothes that i had a hard time going through them or deciding what i wanted to wear. And I also realised that i didn't really like most of what i had bought. Which lead to more buying. The same went for my obsession for gadgets. After a year i had so many iPads and iPhones that i did not know what to do with them that costed my thousands of dollars.

When I woke up one day and looked around my house, i realised that i regretted most of the purchases I made and that all these stuff was actually making me very unhappy.

So I did what made sense to me at the time, I started decluttering.

I went through each and every item in my house from my wardrobe to my bedroom, to my study and living room. And with each item held in my hand i asked myself 3 questions: "do i really need this?" "does this make me happy?" and "can someone else make better use of this item?"

And as i started sorting i realised that 70% of my things were stuff that i do not need and will not use. and only 30% of them actually brought me some sort of joy. The most prominent being the clothes i always wore even when i had countless others to choose from.

As I began donating to salvation army and discarding the junk, my house became less and less messy and cramped. And what remained was not only more space, but things that I had an emotional attachment to. Things that brought me a sense of joy when i loooked at them or touched them. The extra space also brought me a sense of peace that there were no hidden junk in cupboards and the space I had could put to better use rather than housing useless things.

This decluttering process was not only therapeutic but necessary for me. For the first time i felt that having lesser things actually made me happier. And That i didnt have to spend my way to achieve happiness. I also realised that what I had already in my house was more than I would ever need and that this is my sacred space that i should only fill with things that are meaningful to me.

What changed for me is that these days when i go shopping, I don't have the urge to spend money on things just because anymore. I end up gravitating towards shops that sells plants, fishes because those are what brings me joy these days. Living things that I have to care for with love and dedication.

This change in wanting lesser things has not only made me happier but also saved me money in the process.

I just want to end off by saying that having more things will never make you happy, but making more friends and being grateful for what you already have can give u the happiness you have been searching for.

Chapter 3:

Take Ownership of Yourself

What belongs to you but is used by other people more than you?

Your name.

And that's okay. People can use your name. But you must never allow yourself to lose ownership of you. In fact, you need to be incredibly conscious of taking ownership of everything that you are. And I do mean everything. Those few extra pounds, the nose you think is too big, your ginger hair or freckled skin. Whatever it is that you are insecure about, it's time that you showed up and took ownership. Because the moment you do your world will change.

But what does that look like? Why does it matter?

If someone parks a limo in the road outside your house, hands you the keys and tells you it is yours, what would you do? You're not just gonna put the keys in the ignition and leave it in the road. You are going to put that thing in a garage and get it insured. You will make sure that it is in a place where it is safe from weather and your jealous neighbour. Those are the things that you do when you take ownership of something. You make sure that they are protected because you value them. Then when you drive around town you don't look around as if you've stolen the thing. You drive with style and confidence. You are bold and comfortable because it belongs to you. *That* is what ownership looks like.

Now I know what you're thinking. That's easy to do with a limo, but I what I have is the equivalent of a car built before world war two. But the beautiful thing about ownership is that it does not depend on the object. It is not the thing being owned that you have to worry about, all you have to do is claim it. You've seen teenagers when they get their first car. Even if it is an old rust-bucket they drive around beaming with pride. Why? Because they know that what they have is theirs. It belongs to them and so they take ownership of it.

You have to do the same. You must take ownership of every part of you because in doing so you will keep it secure. You no longer have to be insecure about your weight if you know that that is where you are at right now. That doesn't mean you don't work for change though. It doesn't give you an excuse for stagnancy. You take accountability for your change and growth as much as you do for your present state. But in taking ownership you work towards polishing your pride, not getting rid of your low self-esteem. The difference may sound semantic, but the implications are enormous. The one allows you to work towards something and get somewhere good. The other makes it feel like you are just running away from something. And when you are running away then the only direction that matters is away – even if that means you run in circles.

Make a change today. Own yourself once more and be amazed at the rush that comes with it. With ownership comes confidence.

Chapter 4:

Share Your Troubles Freely and Openly

Life is hard. We go through tons of challenges, problems, and obstacles every single day. We accumulate problems and stresses left right and Center. Absorbing each impact blow for blow.

Over time, these impacts will wear us down mentally and physically. Without a proper release channel, we find that our emotions spill over in ways when we least expect it. We get easily irritated, have a hard time falling asleep, have mood issues, and find ourselves even being temporarily depressed at times.

When we bottle negativity, it festers inside us without us realising what we have done. That is where releasing those tensions by pouring our heart and soul into friends, writing, journaling, and other outlets that allow us to express our feelings freely without judgement.

We may not all have friends that we can truly count on to share our deepest darkest secrets for fear that they might share these secrets unsuspectingly. If we do have these types of friends, treasure them and seek them out regularly to share your problems. By bouncing ideas off someone, we may even find a new solution to an old problem that we couldn't before. The other party may also be able to see things more objectively and with a unique perspective that is contrary to yours which you could potentially use to your advantage.

If writing things down is something that helps you cope with life, then by all means take a piece of paper and write down all the things that have been bothering you.

Journal it, archive it. You may even write a song about it if that helps you process things better. Writing things down help us clear our minds and lets us see the big picture when we come back to it at a later date should we feel ready to address it. When things are too crazy, we may not have the mental capacity to handle everything being thrown at us at one go. So take the time to sort those feelings out.

You may also choose to just find a place that brings you relaxation. Whether it be going to the beach, or renting a hotel, or even just screaming at the top of your lungs. Let those feelings out. Don't keep it hidden inside.

IF all these things still don't work for you, you may want to try seeking help from a professional counsellor or therapist who can work out these issues you have in your life one by one. Never be afraid to book an appointment because your mental health is more important than the stigma associated with seeing a professional. You are not admitting you have a problem, you are simply acknowledge that there are areas in your life that you need assistance with. And that it is perfectly okay and perfectly normal to do so. Counsellors have the passion to serve, the passion to help, and that is why they chose that profession to being with. So seek their assistance and guidance as much as you need to.

Life isn't easy. But we can all take a conscious effort to regulate our emotions more healthily to live a long and balanced life.

Chapter 5:

How To Succeed In Life

"You can't climb the ladder of success with your hands in your pocket."

Every day that you're living, make a habit of making the most out of it. Make a habit of winning today. Don't dwell on the past, don't worry about the future. You just have to make sure that you're winning today. Move a little forward every day; take a little step every day. And when you're giving your fruitful efforts, you're making sure you're achieving your day, then you start to built confidence within yourselves. Confidence is when you close your eyes at night and see a vision, a dream, a goal, and you believe that you're going to achieve it. When you're doing things, when you're productive the whole day, then that long journey will become short in a matter of time.

Make yourself a power list for each day. Take a sheet of paper, write Monday on top of it and then write five critical, productive, actionable tasks that you're going to do that day. After doing the task, cross it off. Repeat the process every day of every week of every month till you get closer to achieving your goals, your dreams. It doesn't matter if you're doing the same tasks every day or how minor or major they are; what matters is that it's creating momentum in things that you've believed you couldn't do. And as soon as the momentum gets completed, you start to believe that you can do something. You eventually stop writing your tasks down because now they've become your new habits. You need a reminder for them. You don't need to cross them off because you're going to do them. The power list helps you win the day. You're stepping out of your comfort zone, doing something that looks uncomfortable for starters, but while doing this, even for a year, you will see yourself standing five years from where you're standing today.

Decide, commit, act, succeed, repeat. If you want to be an inspiration to others, a motivator to others, impact others somehow, you have to self-evaluate certain perceptions and think that'll help you change the way you see yourself and the world. Perseverance, hard-working, and consistency would be the keywords if one were to achieve success in life. You just have to keep yourself focused on your ultimate goal. You will fall a hundred times. There's always stumbling on the way. But if you have the skill, the power, the instinct to get yourself back up every time you fall, and to dig yourself out of the whole, then no one can stop you. You have to control the situation, Don't ever let the situation control you. You're living life exactly as it should be. If you don't like what you're living in, then consider changing the aspects. The person you are right now versus the person you want to be in the future, there's only a fine line between the two that you have to come face-to-face with.

Your creativity is at most powerful the moment you open your eyes and start your day. That's when you get the opportunity to steer your emotions and thoughts in the direction that you want them to go, not the other way around. Every failure is a step closer to success. We won't succeed on the first try, and we will never have it perfect by trying it only once. But we can master the art of not giving up. We dare to take risks. If we never fail, we never get the chance of getting something we never had. We can never taste the fruits of success without falling. The difference between successful people and those who aren't successful is the point of giving up.

Success isn't about perfection. Instead, it's about getting out of bed each day, clearing the dust off you, and thinking like a champion, a winner, going on about your day, being productive, and making the most out of it. Remember that the mind controls your body; your body doesn't hold your mind. You have to make yourself mentally tough to overcome the fears and challenges that come in the way of your goals. As soon as you get up in the morning, start thinking about anything or anyone that you're grateful for. Your focus should be on making yourself feel good and confident enough to get yourself through the day.

The negative emotions that we experience, like pain or rejection, or frustration, cannot always make our lives miserable. Instead, we can consider them as our most incredible friends that'll drive us to success. When people succeed, they tend to party. When they fail, they tend to ponder. And the pondering helps us get the most victories in our lives. You're here, into another day, still breathing fine, that means you got another chance, to better yourself, to be able to right your wrongs. Everyone has a more significant potential than the roles they put themselves in.

Trust yourself always. Trust your instinct—no matter what or how anyone thinks. You're perfectly capable of doing things your way. Even if they go wrong, you always learn something from them. Don't ever listen to the naysayers. You've probably heard a million times that you can't do this and you can't do that, or it's never even been done before. So what? So what if no one has ever done it before. That's more of the reason for you to do it since you'll become the first person to do it. Change that 'You can't' into 'Yes, I definitely can.' Muhammad Ali, one of the greatest boxers to walk on the face of this planet, was once asked, 'how many sit-ups do you do?' to which he replied, 'I don't count my sit-ups. I only start counting when it starts hurting. When I feel pain, that's when I start counting because that's when it really counts.' So we get a wonderful lesson to work tirelessly and shamelessly if we were to achieve our dreams. Dr. Arnold Schwarzenegger beautifully summed up life's successes in 6 simple rules; Trust yourself, Break some rules, Don't be afraid to fail, Ignore the naysayers, Work like hell, And give something back.

Chapter 6:

Overcoming Your Fears

Today we're going to talk about the topic of fears. What fear is and how we can overcome it. Now before we dive into it, let us just take a brief moment to think of or right down what our greatest fears are right now.

Whether it be taking the next step in your relationship, fear of the unknown, fear of quitting your job and not finding another one, fear or death, fear of illnesses, whatever fear that jumps out at you and is just eating at you at the back of your mind, i want you to remember that fear as we go through this video.

So what is fear exactly? Whilst there are many definitions of fear out there, I'm going to take, as usual, my spin on things. And to me fear is simply a negative feeling that you assign to usually a task that you really don't want to do. And most of the time, the fear is of the unknown, that you can't visualise what is going to happen next. You don't know whether the outcome will be good or bad, and you don't know whether it is the right move to make. So this trio of thoughts keep circling round and round and eventually you just decide that you are not going to take any action on it and you just shove it to one side hoping that it goes away. And whilst you may do that temporarily, sometimes even for months, one day you are going to have to come face to face with it again. And when that day comes, you will either be paralysed again or you may again put it off to a later date.

We procrastinate on our fears because we want a sure thing. We want to know what will happen next, and we fear what we don't know.

Now for the fears that we are talking about today, it is something that will affect your life if u don't take action. If it is like a fear of bungee jumping or sky driving, sure that fear is physical and very real, but also you can make a choice not to do it and your problem is solved. It will not affect your life in a negative way if u don't do it.

But if it is a fear of a career switch because you already hate your job so much and are totally miserable, that is a fear that you should do your best to try and address as soon as possible.

So what can and should you do about these sorts of fears? The answer for this one is not going to be that difficult. Simply think of the consequences of not conquering your task and how much it might prevent you from moving forward in life and you have got your answer.

When the pain associated with not accomplishing the task becomes greater than the fear we assign to it, it is the tipping point that we need to finally take that action. But instead of waiting to get to that excruciating pain, we can visualise and project what it could potentially feel like if we don't do it now and the pain we might feel at a later day, say 1 year from now, when we have wasted another full year of our life not taking that leap of faith, the time we have burned, the time we can never get back, and the opportunity cost of not taking action now, we might just decide that we don;t want to wait until that day comes and face that huge amount of regret that we should've done something a lot sooner.

And what we need to simply do is to just take action. Taking action is something you will hear from all the gurus you will find out there. When faced with a fear or challenge, instead of wondering what dangers lurk in the unknown, just take action and let the experience tell you whether it was indeed the right or wrong decision. Do you necessary homework and due diligence beforehand and take that calculated step forward instead of procrastinating on it. Life is too short to be mucking around. Just go for it and never live your life in fear or regret ever again.

I challenge each and everyone of you to go through the list that we have created at the start of the video. The one that you have been most fearful of doing. And i want you to assess the pros and cons of each fear that you have written down. If there are more pros than cons, i want you to set a deadline for yourself that you will take action on it. And that deadline is today. Don't waste precious time worrying and instead spend more time doing.

I hope you learned something today and as always take care and i wish you all the best in overcoming your fears and achieving your goals as fast as possible. See you in the next one.

Chapter 7:

Motivate Yourself

Motivation is a multibillion dollar industry.

There are many great motivational materials to help keep you motivated.

Some of the motivational material is great and should be studied and applied but this kind of motivation is what I call push, which is a good start, but in combination with pull motivation,(your personal why and reason), you can reach your goals faster.

With the use of videos, books , audio material and concentrating on your reasons, the sky really is the limit.

Using what works for you, which may be different than what works for others.

Motivation is very much personal to you.

Work with what pulls you and pushes you to reach your goals on record time.

Pushing and pulling everyday until your dream becomes reality.

The pull is your WHY , the big reason for taking action in the first place.

The pull is the motivations that effect you personally, and the big fire that will help your dream burn , even through the storms and the rain.

Using the push motivators in conjunction to maximize your motivation on all fronts.

Create as much of your dream around you as you can with what you have right now to make it seem more real.

Pictures , music , videos, foods, smells , clothing.

Whatever you can do to create it now.

The engine to drive you there may not have arrived yet, but don't close the factory, work on the interior and bodywork, because your engine is on the way.

You know what you want, you know the first steps, take them in confidence, not fear.

If the dream is here, it is already real if you just believe and move towards it.

With motivation , self determination and faith you have already won the race before it has even begun.

Setting up the ideal environment for the garden of your life to flourish.

Strengthen the desire, strengthen the belief.

Motivation in the mind without belief in the heart will only lead to disappointment.

Your why must be something close to the heart for you to endure the tribulations of champions.

Your motivations must be clear and personal.

Defining your purpose, often money alone will not make us happy.

The money must have a greater personal purpose to bring you happiness.

Giving often feels more rewarding than recieving.

As living a truthful life is more rewarding than decieving.

The key to your dreams is often what you are believing.

Believing in yourself and your capabilities is key.

You can study every bit of motivational material ever made, but if you don't believe in yourself, you can not be successful.

Self belief and self motivation are far stronger than the push of what we can learn from the outside.

Let the outside information light the fire as it is intended, be a keen learner of what is relevant, and motivate yourself by concentrating on what is important to you.

Motivate yourself , health, happiness and wealth.

Its possible for you now.

If you believe and push to achieve.

Chapter 8:

Gravitational Leadership

Leadership.

It's not about position it is about disposition. It is not a title it is a role. A role you can take on from any place. Even if you are at the lowest point in the hierarchy – you can still lead. Leadership is not about being on the top rung, it is about holding ladders for others. It is not about having the most authority either. When a battalion went on a mission authorised by the King, the battalion did not have the King's authority, only his approval. Yet within them someone could still rise and lead the others. The beginning of your leadership is making decisions and taking action that gets approved by the people in authority. In doing that you will get noticed and over time trusted as an advisor. Sometimes the way you think and conduct yourself will enable you to lead people above you before you get any opportunity to lead people below you.

Because leadership is gravity.

Gravity does not push us downwards. It is not a force that comes from above us and holds us back.

Firstly, gravity does not push it pulls. Pulling involves leading by example and drawing people to you by virtue of your character. The good decisions that you make, the beneficial actions that you take, start to bundle together as a mass of admirable quality under your name. And gravity is just a reflection of mass. The more you engage and go all-in the faster that mass will grow – and with it your gravity will.

But gravity is not just something that attracts the people below you. Gravity doesn't pull downwards on a 2D plane, it pulls towards a centre. The people who are on the same level as you should be led by you as well. Not only that but you should be influencing the people above you. Not in such a way that you suck up to them but in a way that you stand out. Not necessarily even with the intention of climbing the ladder. Leadership must always be about leading in the space that you are without leaning towards the space you want to be. Allow promotions or advancements to flow naturally – if you try to force them then you will be detracting from your gravity and ultimately end up worse off.

Lastly, gravity does not hold people back, it keeps them grounded. Gravity is the force that enables us to walk forward, to move while retaining control. People who have been to space can testify to the lack of control experienced without gravity and the dangers therein. The markings of a leader is someone who is able to keep people grounded to the mission while still giving them freedom of movement. Gravity does not inhibit progress it gives it a better framework to work within. It allows people to pursue things with passion while staying within the borders of a greater purpose.

Such is the makings of a leader.

Chapter 9:

Only Buying Things that serve a purpose For you

Today I'm going to talk about the right way to buy things. The right way to shop. The right way to spend your hard earned money.

You see, many of us think that we need to buy things to make working hard at our jobs worth the effort. Sure it does help, in the form of retail therapy for some, but a lot of times we end up just excessively buying things that clutter up our house, our space, our homes. Stuff that we only use once and never touch again. Clothes is a common way that this kind of hoarding happens. We don't notice it because we are buying one shirt or one pants at a time, but over just a few shopping sprees and we find our closets full to the brim. And we never wear some of these clothing's more than once, but we throw the "old" ones to make way for the new.

I believe that the right way to buy things is only to purchase quality items that truly deserve a spot in our homes. Things that bring us joy. Things that we are 1000% sure we will use regularly.

For me, I love apple products. I admit that this one area is where I spend most of my money. I may not buy clothes, shoes, bags, but i will definitely put down money to buy apple products. The thing though is that I only buy items that serve a purpose for me in everyday things that I do. As a music lover, i loved their audio products and the ease of which I can enjoy my favourite music and tv shows with their devices. And I use these products on a daily basis. Everytime i pick up an apple product, i find it such a joy to use.

If you get that same feeling with a particular item, it is okay to get it. I'm not here to tell you u shouldnt be buying anything. As long as it is within your means and you know it will not end up untouched for months, then by all means get it. If something doesn't serve you anymore, sell it, donate it away, keep your space free of clutter.

A clutter-free home can provide enormous benefits for our mental and emotional health. To quote Marie Kondo, and to go one step further, only buy things that truly spark joy in you. Never buy things just because. You may feel good in the moment to splurge, but that feeling won't last. Pick your battles and pick your items carefully.

Chapter 10:

You're Good Enough

People come and say 'I did something stupid today. I am so bad at this. Why is it always me?' You will acknowledge even if no one else says it, we often say it to ourselves.

So what if we did something stupid or somewhat a little awkward. I am sure no one tries to do such things voluntarily. Things happen and sometimes we cause them because we have a tendency to go out of our way sometimes. Or sometimes our ways have a possibility of making things strange.

It doesn't make you look stupid or dumb or ugly or less competent. These are the things you make up of yourself. I am not saying people don't judge. They do. But their judgment should not make you think less of yourself.

No matter how much you slip up, you must not stop and you must not bow down to some critique. You only have to be a little determined and content with yourself that you have got it alright.

You need to realize your true potential because no matter what anyone says, you have what it takes to get to the top.

Need some proof? Ask yourself, have you had a full belly today? Have you had a good night's sleep last night? Have you had the will and energy to get up and appear for your job and duties? Have you had the guts to ask someone out to dinner because you had a crush on them?

If you have a good answer to any of these questions, and you have done it all on your own with your efforts. Congratulations my friend, you are ready to appraise yourself.

You have now come to terms with your abilities and you don't need anyone else's approval or appraisal. You don't depend on anyone either psychologically or emotionally.

So now when the times get tough you can remind yourself that you went through it before. And even if you failed back then, you have the right energy and right state of mind to get on top of it now. You are now well equipped to get ahead of things and be a better person than you were the last time.

You are enough for everything good or not so good happening in and around you.

Your health, your relations, your carrier, your future. Everything can be good and better when you have straightened out your relationship with yourself. When you have found ways to talk to yourself ad make yourself realize your true importance. When you learn to admire yourself.

Once you learn to be your best critic, you can achieve anything. Without ever second-guessing yourself and ever trying to care for what anyone else will think.

If you find yourself in a position where you had your heart broken but you still kept it open, you should have a smile on your face. Because now you might be on your path to becoming a superior human being.

7 Ways On How To Attract Success In Life

Successful people fail more times than unsuccessful people try. A new thought author and metaphysical writer Florence Scovel Shinn in her timeless 1940 novel, 'the secret door to success,' suggests that "Success is not a secret, it is a system." Throughout the centuries, the leaders have alluded to the possibility that success can be attracted into one's life simply by thinking and doing. It is rather a planned journey as we give validity to the premise of creating a plan or setting a goal for ourselves. Goals are set to be achieved, and achievements pave the way for success. Here are 7 Ways To Attract Success In Your Life:

1. Define What Success Means To You

Success is subjective to the person who seeks to obtain it, and the ideas may be different for each other. For some of us, success means wealth. For some, it means health and happiness. While for some, it is the mere effort of getting out of bed every day. But the thing that is most highlighted is that we can never get success without struggling. Every one of us wants success, but we do not know how to bring about that life-changing phenomenon that will take us to the zenith of our potential.

2. Begin with Gratitude:

From flying to the sky to crashing to the ground, be always thankful to wherever life takes you. Always start by being grateful for what you already have. Whether it's good or bad, we cannot climb the stairs of success without having experiences. If we make mistakes, we should make sure not to give up, rather learn from those mistakes. We must strive to embrace our flaws and imperfections. If we tend to fall seven times, we must have the energy to get up eight times. Whatever life throws us at, no matter the obstacles and challenges, we should always be in a state of gratitude and always be thankful for our learning.

3. Stop making excuses:

Your decisions lead to your destiny. If you are thinking about delaying your work or 'chilling' first, then someone else will take that opportunity for himself. You either grab on the opportunities from both hands, or you sit on the sidelines and watch someone else steal your spotlight. There's no concept of resting and being lazy when you have to work towards your goals and achieve your dreams. One of the major mistakes of unsuccessful people is that they make endless excuses. They would avoid their tasks in any way instead of working on them and actually doing them. You will attract success only if you put your mind towards something and work hard towards it.

4. Realize your potential:

The fine line between incredibly hardworking people and yet fail to achieve success, and the ones who are at the peak of their respective field is simple – potential. We never realize our true potential until we are put in a situation where there's no way out but to express our abilities. We might think that people have more excellent skills than us or have more knowledge than us. But the truth is, we have more potential inside of us. This might be tougher to implement as we don't know how well we can handle things while stressing out or how much hidden talents and skills we possess. Our potential is merely what might make us successful or a failure. It all depends on how much we are willing to try and push ourselves forward.

5. Celebrate the success of others:

What you wish upon others finds its way and comes back to you again. While seeing people being successful in their professional and personal lives and making a fortune in their careers and businesses can be tough on our lives, always remember that they too faced struggles and challenges before reaching here. There's no need to be envious as life has an abundance of everything to offer to everyone. Whatever is it in your destiny will always find its way to you. You can't snatch what others have achieved, and similarly, others can't seize whatever that you have or may achieve. Congratulate people around you and be excited for them. Send out positive vibes to everyone so you may receive the same.

6. Behave as if you are successful:

Have you heard of the term "fake it till you make it?" Well, it applies to this scenario too. You can fake your success and act like a successful person until you really become one. First, surround yourself with lucrative people. See what habits they have developed over time, how they dress up, how they behave, and, most importantly, how much work they do daily to achieve their goals. Get inspired from them and adopt their healthy habits. Be successful in your own eyes first so that eventually you can be successful in other's eyes as well.

7. Provide value for others:

While money and fame are the most common success goals, we should first try to focus on creating value in the world. A lot of successful people wanted to change things in the world first and help people out. Mark Zuckerberg built a tool for Harvard students initially and now has over 1.4 billion users. The first thing on our mind after waking up shouldn't be money or success, and it would be to create value for the world and the people around us.

Conclusion:

It would be best if you strived to explore the unique, endless possibilities within you. Then, when you start working on yourself, you're adding to your mind's youth, vitality, and beauty.

PART 2

Chapter 1:

How To Take Note of Your Flaws

We all have flaws. As much as we can try to pretend we are perfect, we will find out soon enough from life that we all have parts of us that fall short in one way or another.

This doesn't mean that we are inferior, rather that we have room for improvement. By reframing our flaws as areas of growth, we can change the way we see our weaknesses.

But before we can grow, we first need to identify exactly what areas in our lives that we actually need to work on. It is easy for many of us to go through our days without thinking too much about the important aspects that we are failing to address. And when the time comes for us to perform, we wonder why we always come up short.

We then berate ourselves and assume that we are no good or that we are worse than others. All because we were not acute and aware enough to work on our flaws consistently over a period of time.

If health is an issue for us, either because we feel we are not getting to our ideal weight or sugar level, or whatever it may be, we need to note the habits that are bringing us down and work to replace them with healthier ones that bring us good instead.

We do this, again, by the power of journaling. Only through journaling can we realize exactly how much we are eating, how many calories we are actually consuming each meal, and how can we replace or reduce our intake to reach our goals.

It is easy for us to assume each meal is independent of the other. But everything we consume adds up. A can of coke might not seem much in one sitting, but 3 cans over the course of the day can quickly add up.

By journaling each activity we are doing, writing down the aspects that we excelled at and ones where we fall short at, we can identify the exact mistakes that we are making in order to improve on them gradually each day.

As the saying goes, practice makes perfect. We don't expect to ace the test on the first try, so why should we expect our flaws to be corrected on the second if we do nothing to improve it?

Once we become painfully aware of every single action we are taking, we can then work backwards and deconstruct each activity To find the areas we can work on.

Trust me, Rome isn't built in a day, so taking note and taking action on your flaws is the only way you will see any long-term progress in anything that you do in life. Take care, I believe in you, and I'll see you in the next one.

Chapter 2:

Overcoming Fear and Self-Doubt

The lack of belief most people have is the reason for their failure at even the smallest things in life. The biggest killer of dreams is the lack of belief in ourselves and the doubt of failure.

We all make mistakes. We all have some ghosts of the past that haunt us. We all have something to hide. We all have something that we regret. But what you are today is not the result of your mistakes.

You are here because of your struggles to make those things go away. You are here now with the power and strength to shape your present and your future.

Our mind is designed to take the shape of what we hold long enough inside it. The things we frequently think about ultimately start filling in the spaces within our memory, so we have to be careful. We have to decide whether we want to stay happy or to hold on to the fear we once wanted to get rid of.

The human spirit and human soul are colored by the impressions we ourselves decide to impose.

The reason why we don't want to explore the possibility of what to do is that subconsciously we don't believe that it can happen for us. We don't believe that we deserve it or if it was meant for us.

So here is something I suggest. Ask yourself, how much time in a day do you spend thinking about your dream? How much time do you spend working on your dreams everyday? What books did you read this year? What new skills have you acquired recently? What have you done that makes you worthy of your dream? Nothing?

Then you are on point with your doubt because you don't have anything to show for when the opportunity presents itself.

You don't succeed because you have this latent fear. Fear that makes you think about the consequences of what will happen if you fail even with all the good things on your hand?

I know that feeling but failure is there to teach you one important and maybe the most essential skill life can teach us; Resilience.

You rediscover your life once you have the strength to fight your every fear and every doubt because you have better things on your hand to care for.

You have another dream to pursue. Another horizon awaits you. Another peak to summit. It doesn't matter if you literally have to run to stand still. You got to do what you got to do, no matter the consequences and the sacrifices.

But failing to do what is required of you has no justifiable defense. Not even fear. Because your fears are self-imposed and you already have many wrong things going on for you right now.

Don't let fear be one of them. Because fear is the most subtle and destructive disease So inhale all your positive energies and exhale all your doubts because you certainly are a better person without them.

Chapter 3:

How To Find Your Passion

Today we're going to talk about a topic that i think many of you are interested to know about. And that is how to find your passion.

For many of us, the realities of work and obligations means that we end up doing something we dislike for the money in the hopes that it might buy us some happiness. That sometimes we stop following our passion because maybe it does not exactly pay very well. And that is a fair decision to make.

But today, i hope to be able to help you follow at least one passion project at any point in your life in the hopes that it might help elevate your spirits, give your life more meaning, and help you live each day with a renewed drive and purpose.

You see, the world can be very dull if we chase something that we actually don't really feel attracted to. For example, when we are forced to do something out of sheer dread day in and day out, it will suck the living soul out of us and we will tend to fall into the trap of running an endless wheel with no hope in sight. When we chase material things for example, money or luxury products, we sell our soul to a job that pays well physically but not emotionally and spiritually. As a human being, we have traded our very essence and time, for a piece of paper or digital currency that serves no purpose than to enrich us externally. While it might feel good to be living comfortably, past a certain threshold, there is a point of diminishing returns. And more money just doesn't bring you that much joy anymore.

Yes you may have the fanciest, car, house, and whatever physical possessions you have. But how many of you have heard stories of people who have a lot of money but end up depressed, or end up blowing it all away because they can never spend enough to satisfy their cravings for physical goods and services. What these people lacked in emotional growth, they tried to overcompensate with money. And as their inner self gets emptier and emptier, they themselves get poorer and poorer as well.

On the flip side, many would argue that passion is overrated. That passion is nothing but some imaginary thing that we tell ourselves we need to have in order to be happy. But i am here to argue that you do not need to make passion your career in order to be happy.

You see, passion is an aspiration, passion is something that excites you, passion is something that you would do even if it does not pay a single cent. That you would gladly trade your time readily for even if it meant u weren't getting anything monetary in return. Because this passion unlocks something within you that cannot be explained with being awarded physical prizes. It is the feeling that you are truly alive and happy, you are so incredibly grateful and thankful to be doing at that very moment in time, that nothing else mattered, not even sleep.

To me, and I hope you will see this too, that passion can be anything you make it out to be. It can be something as simple as a passion for singing, a passion for creating music, a passion for helping others, passion for supporting your family, passion for starting a family, passion for doing charity work, passion for supporting a cause monetarily, or even a passion for living life to the fullest and being grateful each day.

For some lucky ones, they have managed to marry their passion with their career. They have somehow made their favourite thing to do their job, and it fulfills them each day. To those people, i congratulate you and envy you.

But for the rest of us, our passion can be something we align our soul with as long as it fulfils us as well. If we have multiple mouths to feed, we can make our passion as being the breadwinner to provide for our family if it brings us joy to see them happy. If we have a day job that we hate but can't let go off for whatever reasons, we can have a passion for helping others, to use the income that we make to better the lives of others.

And for those who have free time but are not sure what to do with it, to just simply start exploring different interests and see what hobbies you resonate with. You may never know what you might discover if you did a little digging.

What I have come to realize is that passions rarely stay the same. They change as we change, they evolve over time just as we grow. And many of the passions we had when we were younger, we might outgrow them when we hit a certain age. As our priorities in life change, our passions follow along.

In my opinion, you do not need to make your passion your career in order to be truly happy.. I believe that all you need is to have at least 1 passion project at any given point of time in your life to sustain you emotionally and spiritually. Something that you can look forward to on your off days, in your time away from work, that you can pour all your time and energy into willingly without feeling that you have wasted any second. And who knows, you might feel so strongly about that passion project that you might even decide to make it your career some day. The thing is you never really know. Life is mysterious like that.

All I do know is that chasing money for the wrong reasons will never net u happiness. But having a passion, whatever it may be, will keep you grounded and alive.

So I challenge each and everyone of you today to look into your current life, and see there are any bright spots that you have neglected that you could revive and make it your passion project. Remember that passion can be anything you make out to be as long as you derive fulfilment and happiness from it. Helpfully one that isnt material or monetary.

Chapter 4:

Get Motivated Even When You Don't Feel Like It

Have you ever heard of the LOCUS Rule? If you haven't, let me explain it to you. The Locus of control is the aspect of your life in which you come to realize the degree to which you believe you have control over your life and the things revolving around it.

Let's simplify it with an example. Let's say you are presented with a situation where you have to solve a puzzle. When you attempt it, luckily you solve it in record time. Someone comes to you and says that you were able to do it because you are smart.

The next time you are presented with a relatively simpler problem, you spend much more time on it and might not be able to solve some hard ones at all. So you feel demotivated and you don't want to do any more puzzles.

But if you were to spend a considerable time solving the original puzzle while doing calculations and taking educational guesses and thinking a lot. Someone would have pointed out that you are a hard worker, so good Job!

So the next time you would feel more motivated to do any similar job and you might be able to perform better in the next one's.

The first case was determined by an external, unprecedented, immeasurable, God-gifted feat. If at any time, you cannot get something done, you would think that you don't have it in you anymore and you are just a piece of sheer luck.

But if you know for sure that you can achieve absolutely anything, just as you keep doing what you do best, and that being your hard work. Then everything seems achievable and everything seems easy no matter how long it gets.

Life is a balloon stretched over this rule. Life always presents us with opportunities but we miss out on most. We miss out because we have this fear of non-confidence within us. We fear the unknown and so we get stuck in the same old rut of depression, anxiety, and fear.

All these things have a simple initiative for a solution.

You need to be transparent with yourself. You need to prove your strengths and strategies to yourself. And you have to tell it to yourself that you only need a little willpower to always keep one little straw to stick to, for when every support seems to turn to dust.

Look around you. You are still a lot better than the majority. You still have a brain to keep you on your ability to self-analyze.

Think about it. You failed today, but you had some success some time ago. So if you can spend some time feeling sorry for yourself, you can spend the same time trying to put your mind, heart, and body to get up one more time and try one more time.

You might fail again and again and again, but remember that life is not based on one moment of luck. Life is a campaign of hard work followed by dedication and motivation.

Chapter 5:

Feeling That You Don't Have Enough Time

Today we're going to talk about a topic that I think many of us struggle with, myself included. The topic is about feeling that we don't have enough time to do the things that we need to do.

Personally I feel this one a daily basis, and it is partly because of my expectations versus reality. Many a times I set unrealistic expectations of how much time is required to do a particular task on my list that I tend to pack my schedule with way too many items. This leads me to feeling incredible overwhelm and stress because it just doesn't seem like I can get all my objectives down before 12am. We tend to underestimate the amount of time and energy that working on our goals require of us that many times we end up setting ourselves up for failure.

I would watch the clock go by minute by minute, hour by hour, only to find myself still working on the very first task on my list of 10 things to do. As you can already imagine I end up feeling that I'm not being productive, even though most of the time I am, and this feeling that I'm not doing things fast enough erodes my motivation further.

There are times when I am genuinely unproductive - like when I get lost in watching television, browsing the web, playing with my dog, being distracted for the sake of procrastination, and a myriad of reasons. But for the purposes of this topic, I will not be addressing those issues. I want to turn our attention to what we can actually accomplish if given enough time, assuming our level of productivity isnt affected by distractions.

The first thing we have to realise is that the things that we need to get done will take however long it needs to get done. Many times we may not be able to control or accurately measure the duration that a task may take. Instead of setting a time limit on a task, we should instead measure our productivity and be focused on doing rather than completing.

As an entrepreneur, I've come to learn that my work never ends. When I think I have finished one task, another one just comes crashing onto my desk like a meteor - another fire I have to put out, another problem I have to solve. I've come to realise that once I set a deadline for the time I need to complete something, rarely will I ever get it done on time. Most often I will be off by a long shot - either by the hours or even days.

Instead of setting arbitrary number of hours, I found that what worked best for me was to simply let my productivity flow. That I actually do more and accomplish more when I stop worrying about time itself - that I give my work however long it needs to get done and then call it a day.

This has allowed me to not be stressed that I never feel like I don't have enough time. Because in reality, time is relative. Time is something that I assign meaning to. If I simply focus on my designation, my 10 year plan, all I need to do is to simply work hard each day and that'll be good enough for me.

Right now the only thing that makes me feel like I don't have enough time, is when I actually waste them doing nothing meaningful. Having struggled with procrastination all my life, I've come to find out that I am not an innate workaholic. It doesn't come natural to me to want to do the work and that is what is causing me to feel like time is slipping away from me sometimes. That is something I have to continuously work on.

With regards to what you can learn from this - instead of racing against time to complete something, let the work flow out of you like water. Get into a state where productivity oozes out of you. Use a time tracking app to measure the amount of time that you have spent on working. Decide how much time you are willing to set aside to do your work and commit to that time. If 8 hours is the ideal, ensure that you clock those 8 hours and then end the day proud of yourself that you had already done what you set out to do at the start of the day. Never feel like you must do more and never beat yourself up for it. Be nicer to yourself as life is already hard enough as it is.

Another tip that I can recommend that has worked for me is to set a list of the top 3 things you want to do at the start of your day. Instead of the 10 that I did previously that caused me so much stress and anxiety, I have found that 3 is the ideal number of things that will bring us the most satisfaction and the least overwhelm when completing. If we are not able to complete those 3 big tasks, at least maybe we have done 1 or 2. We won't beat ourselves that we hadn't done those other 8 things at the back.

If on the other hand we have successfully completed all those 3 things by mid-day, we may choose to add another 3 items on our list. That way the carrot is never too far away and it is easily attainable should we want to add more.

So I challenge each and everyone of you to look into your day with a new set of lens. Set your intentions right at the start of each day and focus on productivity on a focused set of 3 items. Let the work flow out of you and let the task complete its course naturally without rushing. Remember that it will take as long as it takes and you will only bring yourself more stress if you set a deadline on it. Use it only as a tool for motivation but nothing else if you must set a deadline. Don't be too hard on yourself. Focus on the journey and don't be overly stressed out by feeling that you're always racing against time.

I hope you learned something today. Take care and I'll see you in the next one.

Chapter 6:

The Lure of Wanting Luxury Items

Have you ever walked by a store and pondered over those LV bags if you were a lady? Secretly hoping that you can get your hands on one of those bags so that you can feel good about yourself when you carry them on your shoulders? Or have you ever glanced at a boutique watch shop if you were a guy hoping that you can get your hands on one of the rolexes which costs north of $10k minimum? That could be the same lust and desire for the latest and greatest cars, apple products, clothing, etc. anything you name it.

You think of saving up a year's worth of salary just to be able to afford one of these things and you see yourself feeling good about it and that you can brag to your friends and show off to people that you have the latest and most expensive product on the market. and you imagine yourself being happy that it is all you will need to stay happy.

I am here to tell you that the lure of owning luxury items can only make you happy to a certain extent. And only if purchasing these things is something of great meaning to you, like achieving a big milestone that you want to commemorate in life. In that instance, walking into that store to purchase that luxury product can be a great experience and of great significance as well. Whether it be a birthday gift to yourself, or commemorating a wedding anniversary, job/career work milestone, or any of that in nature, you will tend to hold these products with great sentimental value and hardly will you ever sell these items should the opportunity arise to make a profit from them (which is generally not the case with most things you buy).

I will argue that when you pick these products to wear from your wardrobe, you will indeed be filled with feelings of happiness, but it is not the product itself that makes you happy, but it is the story behind it, the hard work, the commemorative occasion that you will associate and remember these products for. It will transport you back in time to that place in your life when you made the purchase and you will indeed relive that emotion that took you there to the store in the first place. That to me is a meaningful luxury purchase that is not based on lust or greed, but of great significance.

But what if you are just someone who is chasing these luxury products just because everyone else has it? When you walk down the street and you see all these people carrying these products and you just tell yourself you have to have it or else? You find all the money you can dig from your savings and emergency fund to pay for that product? I would argue that in that instance, you will not be as happy as you thought you would be. These kinds of wants just simply do not carry the weight of any importance. And after feeling good for a few days after you owned that luxury good, you feel a deep sense of emptiness because it really does not make you a happier person. Instead you are someone trying to have something but with that comes a big hole in your wallet or your bank account. The enthusiasm and excitement starts to fade away and you wonder whats the next luxury good you need to buy to feel that joy again.

You see, material goods cannot fill us with love and happiness. Luxury goods are only there to serve one purpose, to reward you for your hard work and that you can comfortably purchase it without regret and worry that you are left financially in trouble. The lure of many of us is that we tend to want what we can't have. It could also turn into an obsession for many of us where we just keep buying more and more of these luxury goods to satisfy our craving for materialistic things. You will realise one day that the pursuit never ends, the more you see, the more you want. And that is just how our brains are wired.

I have a confession to make, I had an obsession for apple products myself and I always thought I wanted the latest and greatest apple products every year when a new model comes out. And every year apple seems to know how to satisfy my lust for these products and manages to make me spend thousands of dollars every time they launch something new. This addiction i would say lasted for a good 8 years until I recently realised that the excitement ALWAYS fades after a week or two. Sure it is exciting to play with it for a couple of days while your brain gets used to this incredible piece of technology sitting in front of you. But after a week or two, I am left wondering, whats next? I began to realise that what really made me happy was doing what i love, engaging in my favourite hobbies, meeting friends, and just living simply without so many wants in life. When you have less wants, you automatically go into a mindset of abundance. And that is a great feeling to have.

I challenge all of you today to question what is your real motivation behind wanted to buy luxury items. Is it to commemorate a significant achievement in your life? or is it a meaningless lust for something that you want to emulate others for. Dig deeper and you will find the answer. Thank you

Chapter 7:
Put Yourself In Positions of Opportunity

Today I examined a story of a very famous woman in Singapore who had a less than perfect childhood, but grew up to become a big personality in the media industry. The woman I am fascinated today is the artiste known as Sharon Au.

You see, Sharon was a child of divorced parents. She moved from home to home, staying with relatives up until she was 17. Her parents were never really there for her but she had something special in her. She was resilient and she always strived to be the best.

While she did not intend to be a famous personality, she auditioned for a role as a dancer in a musical after having seen it many times before on stage, learning the songs word for word. This immediately impressed the auditioner who casted her the role of the lead.

Now we have our first example of how she had placed herself in a position of opportunity and got herself a start in what would be a lucrative career as a media personnel. The first takeaway is that she dared to try. She dared to audition. And she dared to challenge herself to be placed in a role where she could further showcase her talents. This was her at age 20.

With this first opened door, she and her cast in the musical managed to sell out 16 shows. And as luck would have it once again, she made a remarkable performance on one of the show nights while a big head of a media executive company was there to watch. She was offered a contract immediately and from there her media career took off.

She subsequently appeared in countless tv shows and became a prominent tv personality in the Singapore media industry. As her fame and popularity escalated, so did the number of opportunities in the form of contracts and endorsements that followed. She subsequently became so popular that she won numerous awards and accolades for her performance as a host and actress.

After spending more than 10 years in the media industry, she decided to pursue her initial dream of going to university at age 30. She left her lucrative entertainment career in Singapore for a university in Japan and appeared on the deans list multiple times while impressively studying and completing her education in a foreign language. She is now currently a investment director working in Paris.

I just want to impress on you today on how one decision in her life, to audition for a role in a musical, let to a chain of events that brought her much successes in her very fulfilling yet ever changing career in work and life. She had effectively placed herself in a position of opportunity one time which had led to multiple opportunities and doors opening for her like a floodgate. Barring her talent and tireless work ethic that should inspire everyone should you dig deeper into her life and career, she remains a gem in Singapore's history as an icon who had left a mark on the entertainment history even till this day.

I want to challenge all of you to not give up in placing yourself in areas where opportunities can present themselves to you. You might not know when or how it might hit you, but when it does, it can come so fast and so great that you better be prepared for it.

I hope you all enjoyed the sharing today and i hope you learned something new to improve your life and situation. As always see you in the next one.

Chapter 8:

Who Are You Working For?

Who you work for is up to you,

but ultimately every person has a choice in that decision.

Whether you are self-employed, self-made, or salaried,

You determine your own destiny.

As Earl Nightingale said, only the successful will admit it.

You might work for one company your whole life,

but ultimately you are still working for yourself and your family.

If you do not like the practices of your company,

you have the power to leave and make a change.

You must choose to serve who you believe to be worthy of your life.

High self-esteem stops successful people ever feeling subordinate to anyone.

Achieve your goals by envisioning yourself providing quality service in the companies

and places that will maximise your chances of success.

Always view yourself as equal to everybody.

All of us have unique talents and qualities within us.

Acknowledg that we can learn from anybody.

Nobody is above or below us.

You can build such qualities that are keys to success.

If one client is taking all your time, reassess his or her value.

If the contract is no longer rewarding, end it as soon as possible.

Doesn't matter if it is a business or personal relationship.

You must get clear on the fact that you are working for you.

You should consider no one your boss.

You should view whoever pays you as a client,

As such you should provide them the best service you can.

Always look to create more opportunity for your business.

Don't look for security - it doesn't exist.

Even if you find it for a time, I guarantee it will be boring at best.

Look for productivity and progression.

Change is definite. It is the only constant.

It will be up to you whether it is progression or regression.

Work with people who have similar goals and objectives.

You should always work with, never for.

Remember that you are always working for yourself.

If working with a company is not bringing you any closer to your goal,

End it now and find one that will.

You should never feel stuck in a job because leaving it is only a letter or phone call away.

You can replace that income in a million different ways.

If you don't like someone scheduling your week for you, start your own business.

If you don't know how, get the training.

Investing in your skills is an investment in your future.

Learning doesn't end with high school.

That was only the beginning – that was practice

Be a life-long learner.

Learn on the job.

Learn so you can achieve more.

Once you admit that you are working for you,

change your bosses title to 'client'.

Open your eyes to a world of other big and wonderful opportunities.

Realize that you are more valuable than you previously believed yourself to be.

Believe you will are incredibly valuable, and you deserve to be paid accordingly.

Whether you are a minimum wage worker or a company director,

you probably haven't even scratched the surface of your capabilities.

Every time someone places limits on what is possible, somebody proves them wrong.

You work for yourself, the possibilities are limitless.

Chapter 9:

Practicing Visualisation For Your Goals

Today we're going to talk about visualisation and why I think all of you should practice some form of visualisation everyday to help keep you on track to the future that you can see yourself living in maybe 5 or 10 years down the road.

So before we begin today's video, i want you to write down some of the goals that you want to achieve. These goals need not be entirely monetary, it could also be finding a partner, having a kid, having lots of friends, playing in a tournament of some elite sport, playing fluent guitar, skateboarding like a pro, or even working at the Apple store maybe... any personal goals and dreams that you might think u want.

And In terms of monetary goals, it could be the kind of income level and the kinds of material possessions that you wish you had, for example a dream car of yours, a pretty landed house or apartment in a prestigious neighbourhood, and nice flat screen Tv, a 10k diamond ring. Or whatever it may be. No matter how ridiculous, i want you to write these down.

Alright now that we have got this list in your hands, lets talk about what visualisation is and how it can be a powerful tool to help you actually achieve your goals.

What visualisation essentially is in a nutshell, is that it helps you step into the shoes of your future self, whether that may be 10 mins in the future, 10 years into the future, or even when you are at your death bed.

So why would we want to even think or imagine ourselves in the future when people have been telling us to be present and living in the moment etc. People including myself in my other videos. Well you see, the difference is that with visualisation, we are not looking into our past successes and failures as factors that influence our present state of mind, but rather to create a picture of a person that we want to be in the future that we can be proud of. A person that we think and aspire to become. Whether that be emulating an already rich or successful person, or simply just choosing to see yourself in possession of these things and people that you want in your life. Visualisation can help us mentally prepare ourselves for our future and help us solidify and affirm the actions that we need to take right now at this very moment to get to that end point.

Visualisation is such a powerful tool that when done correctly and consistency, our brain starts to blur the line between our present reality and our future self. And we are able to retrain and rewire our brain to function in the way that helps us achieve those goals by taking action more readily. If we have chosen to visualise ourselves as a pro tennis player, however far fetched it may seem, we have already decided on some level deep down that we are going to become that person no matter what it takes. And on a mental level, we have already committed to practicing the sport daily to achieve that outcome. If it is an income goal we hope to achieve, by visualising the person we hope to become who earns maybe $100k a month, yes it might sound far fetched again, but it is certainly not impossible, we will take actions that are drastically different than what we are doing today to make that goal happen. A person who visualises themselves making $100k a month will say and do things that are completely different from someone who tells themselves that they are okay to make just $2000 a month.

The action and effort taken is on a whole other level. A person who says they want to stay an amateur tennis player will do things differently than someone who visualises themselves becoming the top player of the sport who is ready to win grand slams.

With these two examples in mind, now i want you to take that list that we have created at the start of the video, and i want you to now place yourself inside of your imagination, I want you to start picturing a future you that has already been there done that. A future you who has got everything that he ever wanted, friends, family, money, career, sports, hobbies, travel, seeing the world, all of it. And I want you to visualise how you actually got to that point. What were the actions that you took to get there. How much time did you have to spend on each activity each day, day in and day out, and the level of commitment and desire that you needed to have, the belief that you will and have achieved your wildest dreams, how that must have felt, the emotion associated with reaching your goals, and becoming the person that you've always known you could be.

As this is your first time, i want you to spend at least 5-10mins trying to see yourself in your future shoes. It might not come right away as even visualisation takes practice. When we are so used to not using our imagination, it can be hard to reactivate that part of the brain. If you do not see it right now, i want you to keep going at it daily until that person in your head becomes clearer and clearer to you.

It might be easier to just see yourself as the next Warren Buffet, Jeff Bezos, Steve Jobs, Roger Federer, or whoever idol and superstar you wish to emulate. When you aim to emulate their success, you will mimic the actions that they take, and that could be a good way to start. Even a small change in your attitude and actions can go a long way.

Now that you have had a taste of the power of visualisation, I want you to practice visualisation on a daily basis. Again, everything boils down to consistency, and the more u practice seeing yourself as a successful person in life regularly, the more you believe that you can get there. Try your very best to pair that feeling with immense emotion. The feeling you get when you finally reached the summit. It will give you the best chance of success at actually following through with your goals and dreams.

To keep yourself motivated each day to practice visualisation, click on this link and save it to your favourites of daily habits. Refer to meditation series.

This has been quite an interesting topic to make for me as I have used visualisation myself with great success in helping me take consistent action, something that I struggle with daily, to reprogram my mind to work hard and stay the path.

I hope you learned something today and I wish you all the best in your career and life.

5 Ways To Adopt Right Attitude For Success

Being successful is a few elements that require hard work, dedication, and a positive attitude. It requires building your resilience and having a clear idea of your future ahead. Though it might be hard to decide your life forward, a reasonable manner is something that comes naturally to those who are willing to give their all. Adopting a new attitude doesn't always mean to change yourself in a way but, it has more meaning towards changing your mindset to an instinct. That is when you get stressed or overworked is because of an opposing point of view on life.

With success comes a great sense of dealing with things. You become more professional, and you feel the need to achieve more in every aspect. Don't be afraid to be power-hungry. But, it also doesn't mean to be unfair. Try to go for a little more than before, each step ahead. Make your hard work or talent count in every aspect. Make yourself a successful person in a positive manner, so you'll find yourself making the most of yourself. And don't give up on the things you need in life.

1. Generate Pragmatic Impressions

"The first impression is the last impression." It's true that once you've introduced yourself to the person in front of you, there is only a tiny chance that you'll get to introduce yourself again. So, choosing the correct wording while creating an impression is a must. You need to be optimistic about yourself and inform the other person about you in a way that influences them. An impression that leaves an effect on them, so they will willingly meet you again. A person must be kind and helpful towards its inferior and respectful towards their superior. This is one of the main characteristics for a person to be a successful man or woman. And with a negative attitude, the opposite occurs. People are more inclined to work without you. They nearly never consider you to work with them and try to contact you as little as possible. So, a good impression is significant.

2. Be True To Your Words

Choose your wording very carefully, because once said, it can't be taken back. Also, for a successful life, commitment is always an important rule. Be true to what you said to a person. Make them believe that they can trust you comfortably. So, it would be best if you chose your words. Don't commit if you can't perform. False commitment leads to loss of customers and leads to the loss of your impression as a successful worker. Always make sure that you fulfill your commands and promises to your clients and make them satisfied with your performance. It leads to a positive mindset and a dedication to work towards your goal.

3. A Positive Personal Life

Whatever you may be doing in your professional life can impact your personal life too. Creating the right mindset professionally also helps you to keep a positive attitude at home. It allows you to go forward with the proper consultation with your heart. It will make you happier. You'll desire to achieve more in life because you'll be satisfied with your success. It will push to go furthermore. It will drive you towards the passion for desiring more. Hard work and determination will continue to be your support, and you will be content will your heart. By keeping a good attitude, you'll be helping yourself more than helping others.

4. Be Aggressive and Determined

Becoming goal-oriented is one of the main factors evolving success in your life. If you are not determined to do your work, you'll just accept things the way others present you. It will leave you in misery and deeply dissatisfied with yourself. Similarly, you'll tend to do something more your way if you are goal-oriented and not how others want. You'll want to shale everything according to your need, and you become delighted with yourself and the result of your hard work. Always keep a clear view of your next step as it will form you in to your true self. Don't just go with the flow, but try to change it according to your wants and needs.

5. Create Your Master Plan

Indeed, we can't achieve great things with only hard work. We will always need to add a factor or to in our business. But by imagining or strategizing, some plans might be helpful. With hard work and some solid projects, we will get our desired outcome. If not, at least we get something close. And if you chose the wrong option, then the amount of hard work won't matter. You'll never get what you want no matter the hard work. So, always make sure to make plans strategically.

Conclusion

By keeping a positive attitude, you'll not only be helpful to others but to yourself too. Make sure you keep the proper manner—a manner required to be a successful person. Do lots of achievements and try to prove yourself as much as possible. Try keeping a good impact on people around you in everything you do. Have the spirit and courage to achieve great heights. And be sure to make moat of yourself. Consistency is the key.

Chapter 10:
Don't Overthink Things

Analysis Paralysis, how many of you have heard of this term before? When a decision is placed before us, many of us try to weigh the pros and cons, over and over again, day and night, and never seem to be able to come up with an answer, not even one week later.

I have been guilty of doing such a thing many times in my life, in fact many in the past month alone. What I've come to realize is that there is never going to be a right decision, but that things always work out in the end as long as it is not a rash decision.

Giving careful thought to any big decision is definitely justified. From buying a car, to a house, to moving to another state or country for work, these are big life-changing decisions that could set the course for our professional and financial future for years to come. In these instances, it is okay to take as much time as we need to settle on the right calculated choice for us. Sometimes in these situations, we may not know the right answer as well but we take a leap of faith and hope for the best and that is the only thing we can do. And that is perfectly okay.

But if we translate the time and effort we take in those big projects into daily decisions such as where to go, what to eat, or who to call, we will find ourselves in a terrible predicament multiple times a day. If we overthink the simple things, life just becomes so much more complicated. We end up over-taxing our brain to the point where it does not have much juice left to do other things that are truly important.

The goal is to keep things simple by either limiting your choices or by simply going with your gut. Instead of weighing every single pro and con before making a decision, just go. The amount of time we waste calculating could be better spent into energy for other resources.

I have found that i rarely ever make a right choice even after debating hours on end whether I should go somewhere. Because i would always wonder what if i had gone to the other place instead. The human mind is very funny thing. We always seem to think the grass could be greener on the other side, and so we are never contented with what we have in front of us right here right now.

The next time you are faced with a non-life changing decision, simply flip a coin and just go with the one that the coin has chosen for you. Don't look back and flip the coin the other way unless it is truly what your heart wants. We will never be truly happy with every single choice we make. We can only make the most of it.

7 Ways To Know If You're A Good Person

This question is something that we wonder from time to time. When we are at our lowest point and we look around, there could be a chance that there may not be that many people in our lives that we can really count on.

We start to wonder how people actually see us. Are we good people? Have we been nice to those around us? Or do we come off as pretentious and hence people tend to stay clear of us for some reason.

There is a dilemma lately about the use of social media and having followers. It seems that people are interested in following your socials, but when it comes to you asking them out or chatting them up, they don't respond or are uninterested to meet up with you.

You then start to wonder if there is something wrong with you. You start to question your morals, your self-worth, and everything about your life. This can quickly spiral out of control and lead to feelings that you are somehow flawed.

Today we're going to help you answer that question: Am I a good person? Here are 7 Ways To Find Out If You Are Indeed One

1.   Look At The People Who Have Stuck Around

I think this one is a good place to start for all of us. Instead of wondering if we have gone wrong somewhere, take a look at the friends and family who have stuck around for you over all this time. They are still there for you for a reason. You must have done something right for them not to leave you for other people. Sure some of them may not be as close as they once were, but they are still there. Think about the people who celebrate your birthdays with you, the people who still asks if you want to hang out from time to time, and the people who you can count on in times of emergency. We may not be able to determine if we are good people from this, but we know that at least we are not so far off the rails.

2.   Ask Them To Be Honest With You

If you really want to find out if you are a good person, ask your friends directly and honestly, to point out to you areas that they feel you need to work on. Sometimes we cannot see the flaws and the misguided actions that we portray to the world. People may gradually dislike and drift away from us quietly without telling us why. The people who have stuck around know you best, so let them be brutally honest with you. Take what they have to say as constructive criticism, rather than a personal attack on your character. It is better to know in what areas you lack as a person and to work to improve it, than to go through life obliviously and thinking that there is absolutely nothing wrong with you.

3.   Think About Why Your Friends May Not Respond To Your Messages

Many a times friendships simply run its natural course. As work, relationships, and family come into the picture, it is inevitable that people drift apart over time. If you decide to hit your friends up and they don't respond, don't take it too personally. It could be that maybe you're just not a vital piece of the puzzle in their lives anymore. If their friendships aren't one that you have been cultivating anyway, you may want to consider removing them completely from your lives. Find new people who will appreciate and love you rather than dwell on the past. There may be nothing wrong with you as a person, it's just the cruel nature of time playing its dirty game.

4.   Keeping It Real With Yourself

Do you think that you are a good person? The fact that you are here shows that you may already have an inclination that something may not be quite right with you but you can't quite put a finger on it. Instead of looking for confirmation from external sources, try looking within. Ask yourself the hard questions. Think about every aspect of your life and evaluate yourself. If you have more enemies than friends, maybe there is something you aren't doing quite right that needs some work. Write those possible flaws down and see if you can work through them.

5.   Do You Try Your Best To Help Others?

Sometimes we may not be great friends but we may be great at other things, such as being passionate about a cause or helping other people. Maybe friendships aren't a priority for us and hence it is not a good indicator of whether we are good people by looking at the quality of our friendships. If instead we are driven by a cause bigger than ourselves, and we participate through volunteering, events, and donation drives, we can pat ourselves on the back and say that at least we have done something meaningful to better the lives of others. In my opinion you are already a winner.

6.   Is Life Always About What You Want?

This one could be a red flag because if we create a life that is only centred around us, we are in danger of being self-obsessive. Having the "Me First" attitude isn't something to be proud of. Life is about give and take, and decisions should be made fairly for all parties involved. If you only want to do things your way, or go to places you want, at the expense of the opinions of others, you are driving people away without realising it. Nobody likes someone who only thinks about themselves. If you catch yourself in this position, it may be time to consider a 180 turn.

7.   People Enjoy Being Around You

While this may not be the best indicator that you are a good person, it is still a decent way to tell if you are well-liked and if people enjoy your presence. Generally people are attracted to others who are kind, loyal, trustworthy, and charismatic. If people choose to ask you out, they could find you to be one of those things, which is a good sign that you're not all too bad. Of course you could have ulterior motives for presenting yourself in a well-liked manner, but disingenuity usually gets found out eventually and you very well know if you are being deceitful to others for your own personal gain.

Conclusion

There is no sure-fire way to tell if you are a good person. No one point can be definitive. But you can definitely look at a combination of factors to determine the possibility of that age-old question. The only thing you can do is to constantly work on improving yourself. Invest time and effort into becoming a better person and never stop striving for growth in your character.

PART 3

Chapter 1:

The Struggle With Time

Today we're going to talk about a topic that isn't commonly looked at in depth. But it is one that we might hopefully find a new appreciation for. And that is TIME.

Time is a funny thing, we are never really aware of it and how much of a limited resource it really is until we get a rude awakening. Most commonly when our mortality is tested. Whether it be a health scare, an accident, a death of a loved one, a death of a pet, we always think we have more time before that. That we will always have time to say i love you, to put off the things we always told ourselves we needed to do, to start making that change, to spend time with the people that mean the most to us.

As we go about our days, weeks and months, being bothered and distracted by petty work, by our bosses, colleagues, trying to climb the corporate ladder, we forget to stop and check in on our fiends and family... We forget that their time may be running out, and that we may not have as much time with them as we think we do, until it is too late, and then we regret not prioritising them first. All the money that we made could not ever buy back the time we have lost with them. And that is something we have to live with if we ever let that happen.

The other funny thing about time is that if we don't set it aside for specific tasks, if we don't schedule anything, we will end up wasting it on something mindless. Whether it be browsing social media endlessly, or bingeing on television, we will never run out of things to fill that time with. Can you imagine that even though time is so precious, we willingly sacrifice and trade it in for self isolation in front of our TVs and computers for hours on end. Sometimes even for days? Or even on mobile games. Some being so addictive that it consumes most of our waking hours if we are not careful.

Our devices have become dangerous time wasters. It is a tool Shea its literally sapping the living energy out of us. Which is why some responsible companies have started implementing new features that help us keep track of our screen time. To keep us in check, and to not let our children get sucked into this black hole that we might struggle to climb out of.

I believe the biggest struggle with time that we all have is how to spend it in such a way that we can be happy without feeling guilty. Guilty of not spending it wisely. And I believe the best way to start is to start defining the things that you need to do, and the things that you want to do. And then striking a balance. To set equal amounts of time into each activity so that it doesn't overwhelm or underwhelm you. Spend one hour on each activity each day that you feel will have an impact on your life in a meaningful way, and you can spend your time on television or games without remorse.

So I challenge each of you to make the most of your time. SPending time with loved ones always come first, followed by your goals and dreams, and then leisure activities. Never the other way around. That way you can be at the end of your life knowing that you had not wasted the most precious commodity that we are only given a finite amount of. Money can't buy back your youth, your health, or time with loved ones, so don't waste it.

I believe in each and everyone of you, take care, and as always ill see you in the next one.

Chapter 2:

When It Is Time To Let Go and Move On (Career)

Today we're going to talk about a topic that I hope will motivate you to quit that job that you hate or one that you feel that you have nothing more to give anymore.

For the purpose of this video, we will focus mainly on career as I believe many of you may feel as though you are stuck in your job but fear quitting because you are afraid you might not find a better one.

For today's topic, I want to draw attention to a close friend of mine who have had this dilemma for years and still hasn't decided to quit because he is afraid that he might not get hired by someone else.

In the beginning of my friend's career, he was full of excitement in his new job and wanted to do things perfectly. Things went pretty smoothly over the course of the first 2 years, learning new things, meeting new friends, and getting settled into his job that he thought he might stay on for a long time to come seeing that it was the degree that he had pursued in university. However when the 3rd year came along, he started to feel jaded with his job. Everyday he would meet ungrateful and sometimes mean customers who were incredibly self-entitled. They would be rude and he started dreading going to work more and more each day. This aspect of the job wore him down and he started to realise that he wasn't happy at all with his work.

Having had a passion for fitness for a while now, he realized that he felt very alive when he attended fitness classes and enjoyed working out and teaching others how to work out. He would fiddle with the idea of attending a teacher training course that would allow him to be a professional and certified fitness coach.

As his full time job started to become more of a burden, he became more serious about the prospect of switching careers and pursuing a new one entirely. At his job, realized that the company wasn't generous at all with the incentives and gruelling work hours, but he stayed on as he was afraid he wouldn't find another job in this bad economy. The fear was indeed real so he kept delaying trying to quit his job. Before he knew it 3 years more had passed and by this time he full on dreaded every single minute at his job.

It was not until he made that faithful decision one day to send in his resignation letter and to simultaneously pay for the teacher training course to become a fitness instructor did his fortunes start to change for him. The fortunes in this wasn't about money. It was about freedom. It was about growth. And it was about living.

We all know deep in our hearts when it is time to call it quits to something. When we know that there is nothing more that we can possibly give to our job. That no amount of time more could ever fulfill that void in us. That we just simply need to get out and do something different.

You see, life is about change. As we grow, our priorities change, our personalities change, our expectations change, and our passions and our interests change as well. If we stay in one place too long, especially in a field or in something that we have hit a wall at, we will feel stuck, and we will feel dread. We will feel that our time spent is not productive and we end up feeling hopeless and sorry for ourselves.

Instead when we choose to let go, when we choose to call time on something, we open up the doors for time on other ventures, and other adventures. And our world becomes brighter again.

I challenge each and everyone of you to take a leap of faith. You know deep in your hearts when it is time to move on from your current job and find the next thing. If you dont feel like you are growing, or if you feel that you absolutely hate your job because there is no ounce of joy that you can derive from it, move on immediately. Life is too short to be spending 10 hours of your life a day on something that you hate, that sucks the living soul out of you. Give yourself the time and space to explore, to find some other path for you to take. You will be surprised what might happen when you follow your heart.

I hope you learned something today, take care and I'll see you in the next one.

Consistency Can Bring You Happiness

Happiness is an individual concept.

One man's riches is another man's rubbish.

As humans we are not happy if we do not have a routine, a reason to get up, and a purpose to live.

Without working towards something consistently, we become lost.

We begin to drift.

Drifting with no purpose eventually leads to emptiness.

When we are drifting in a job we hate,

We are trading our future away,

When we inconsistent in our relationships,

Problems are bound to arise.

Choose consistent focus instead.

Figure out exactly what you want and start to change it.

Employ consistent routines and habits that to move you towards your goals.

Consistency and persistence are key to success and happiness.

Without consistent disciplined effort towards what we want, we resign to a life of mediocrity.

Read a book for an hour consistently every single day.

You will become a national expert in 1 year.

In 5 years, a global expert.

That is the power of consistency.

Instead, people spend most of their free time scrolling through social media.

Consistency starts in the mind.

Happy Right Now

Control your thoughts to be positive despite the circumstances.
Nothing in the world can make us happy if we choose not to be.

Choose to be happy now and consistently working towards your goals.
We cannot be happy and successful if we dwell in the day to day setbacks.

We must consistently move like a bulldozer.
We have to keep going no matter what.
Nothing stays in the path of a bulldozer for too long.

In life, no matter where you are, you only ever have two choices.
Choose to stay where you are? Or choose to keep moving?

If where you are is making you happy, then by all means do more of it.
If not. What will? And why?
This should be clear before you take action.
Start with the end in your mind.
Let your body catch-up to it afterwards.
The end result is your what.
The action required is your how.
Concentrate on the what and the how and it will all be revealed soon enough.

Concentrate consistently on what you want for yourself and your family.
Distraction and lack of consistent action is a killer of happiness and success.
Your happiness is the life you want.
Take consistent action towards that life you've always dreamed of.
Commitment and endurance is part of that process.

On earth things need time to nurture and grow.
Everything in life depends on it.
The right conditions for maximum growth.

You can't just throw a seed on the concrete and expect it to grow with no soil and water, Just as you can't simply wish for change and not create the right environment for success.

A seed requires not just consistent sunlight,
But the perfect combination of water and nutrients as well.
You might have given that seed sunlight,
just as you have your dream hope,
But without faith and consistent action towards the goal, nothing will happen.
The seed will still stay a seed forever.

Consistency in thought and action is everything towards happiness.
Nothing can grow without it.
Your success can be measured by your time spent working towards your goals.
If we consistently do nothing we become successful in nothing.
If we have to do something, should it not be something worth doing?

Start doing things that make you happy and fulfilled.
Consistency towards something that makes you happy is key towards lasting success.
Adapt when necessary but remain consistent with the end result in mind.
The path can be changed when necessary but the destination cannot.
Accepting anything less is admitting defeat.

Consistent concentration on the end result can and will be tested.
It however cannot be defeated, unless you quit.
If we remain steadfast in our belief that this is possible for us, it will be possible.
After a while things will seem probable. Eventually it becomes definite.

Continue to believe you can do it despite the circumstances.
Continue despite everyone around you saying you can't do it.

In spite of social status,

in spite of illness or disability,

in spite of age, race or nationality,

know you can do nearly anything if you consistently put all of your mind and body towards the task.

Take the pressure off.

There is no set guideline.

It is what you make of it.

There is no set destination or requirements.

Those are set my you.

The only competition is yourself from yesterday.

If you can consistently outperform that person, your success is guaranteed.

Consistent concentration and action towards your dream is key you your success and happiness.

Chapter 3:
Work Harder Than Everybody Else

Lacking motivation and lacking the drive and will to get up out of our butts to take that step towards making our dreams a reality is one that everyone struggles with, even me. Every single day, I wake up knowing the plan and the steps i need to take to get where I want to be, but i just can't seem to bring myself to do these necessary tasks. It is as if a wall is blocking my mind from wanting to do the work.

That is until i came across an article highlighting the power of just working harder than everybody else in whatever field or industry you are in. That you just work harder than your peers and success will come to you. And in this article, it tells the story of how Kobe Bryant, Jack Ma, Mark Cuban, and many other highly successful CEOs and entrepreneurs have achieved immense wealth and success just by working harder than anyone else.

While this concept may seem simple, it is certainty not as easy as it sounds. Putting hours more than your peers when they could be out there relaxing, enjoying life, partying and what not is a sacrifice that not everyone is willing to make. But it is this insane work ethic that drives these people to levels of success not seen by their peers.

Kobe Bryant puts this the best. With every 4 hours more that he practices more than his peers on the basketball court everyday, it starts to add up and compound in an incredible way that by the 5th year of training, none of his peers would ever be able to catch up to him no matter how hard they trained before every tournament or championship. By the time comes around, Kobe would have clocked in thousands of hours more than his peers in practice, and what he lacks for in talent (which I doubt is a factor), he makes up for in time on the court. And this time is what makes him one of the best players of all time. Putting him in the league of legends such as Michael Jordan.

The takeaway from Kobe's story is that every minute extra that you put in more than your peers will add up in time and put you leaps and bounds better than your competition. This can be applied to any field, whether it be a real estate career, as an investor, a trader, an athlete. Anything you set aside time for, you will gain the knowledge in time. You just have to start believing in the hours that you put in will pay off eventually.

This is a lesson that I have experienced personally as well. Many of us want to achieve happiness and success fast, today, now, but they forget that greatness isn't built in a day. And I realised that many of the things that i became good at took time to nurture. And the hours i put it only started paying off 2 to 3 years from the day I began embarking on that new journey or career. and I expect that my future endeavours will also take time to grow.

It is the same as watering a baby sprout everyday and giving it sunlight and water consistently, it only starts to grow really big by its 2nd or 3rd year being a healthy plant constantly fed with nutrients to ensure it has the best chance of survival and growth.

I challenge you today to work harder than everybody else around you and have an insane work ethic. Grind it out every single day, put in the hours that is necessary until you succeed and work your face off. Dont settle for anything less and remove distractions that suck out your time. If you outwork everyone every single day, you will eventually come out on top no matter how talented your competition might be. Just give it your best and never give up.

I hope you learned something today and are taking the necessary steps to get one step closed to your dreams. I wish you success and happiness. Take care and see you in the next one.

Chapter 4:

Your Work is Good Enough

We, humans, are genetically coded to get mad at people getting better at things than us, if not jealous.

These feelings may not bother us right now, and they might never. But these feelings are a leech on their own. They need one to feel low on their self-esteem and may never get ahead of our selves.

We get caught in a competition that no one else imposed on us but we ourselves decided to step into it.

So what we want is one thing, but what we have and we don't want is a whole new problem. We look at one thing and want it instantly without even weighing it side by side with what we already have.

What you have right now is something you have worked for till now. It is something your fate has chosen for you. This is what might be the best for you. You don't necessarily need something better that you like over what you already have. You just need to come to terms with what you have right now and perfect your craft.

You want something more because you are not content with everything you have and everything you do. It is natural to feel this way. It is normal to want more. But it is never OK to leave a thing incomplete and just because you haven't got a hold of things yet.

Things often seem wrong. We feel like an Impostor every time we come up with something new.

Everything we do seem to be a derivative of something someone else has done because we rarely come across a unique idea these days. And even when we come across one, someone else gets the same epiphany. So we never get ahead of ourselves and compete with what is on our hands.

You already have a lot in your hands to take care of so you don't need to pet more worries. You don't need to feed your brain more weaknesses of yourself than you already have.

We all need to realize a simple fact. The fact is that no matter how much we try to second guess our achievements or failures for that matter, we will always finally come to realize that we were right the first time.

You were RIGHT the FIRST TIME. So you only needed to overcome the fight within you.

The first time we do something good, we instantly know that we have something good going on. But then we try to see through others' eyes and lose our own sight of the bigger goals.

So your work is never based on your luck, but only on your talent and devotion. And if no one steps up to give you a round of applause, you still have your own will and mind to be the best judge and critic of your deed. But you also need to become the biggest mentor and coach of your own vessel. Because no vessel without a knock shows its presence.

Chapter 5:

The Power of Breathing To Reset Your Mind

Breathing is something we often take for granted. The breath is always there where we notice or not, keeping us going, and keeping us alive. Without our breath, our hearts will not have enough oxygen and we will die a very agonising death. Yet many of us forget to take the time out of the day to utilise this powerful tool of breathing mindfully to reset our focus, and to calm ourselves down in times of stress and anxiety.

Throughout the way, we are bombarded with things. Work stuff, people stuff, family stuff, and our minds and hearts begin racing and stay elevated throughout the day. Induced by stress hormones, we find ourselves full of cluttered thoughts and our productivity and focus drops as a result. Without clearing all these negative emotions that are bottled up inside us, we may find ourselves stressed out and unable to relax throughout the day, and even at night as we try to go to sleep.

This is where the power of conscious breathing comes into play. We all have the power and choice to take 30 seconds out of our day each time we feel that we need to settle down our emotions and clear our head.

Everytime you feel like things are getting out of control, simply stop whatever you are doing, close your eyes, and focus on breathing through our noise. Notice the breath that goes in and out of your nostrils as you inhale and exhale deeply.

By redirecting our focus to our breaths, we momentarily stop our automatic thoughts and are forced to direct attention to each intentional inhalation and exhalation. This conscious awareness to our breath serves to calm our nerves in times of volatility. If you don't believe it, try it for yourselves right now.

This technique has worked for me time and time again. Everytime i catch myself feeling distracted or unhappy, i would stop whatever i was doing, put on my noise cancelling earphones with the music turned off, and to just sit in complete silence as i focused on my breath. After about a minute or two, i find myself with a clearer head. A cleanse of sorts. And then i would attend to whatever task i was doing before.

This takes practice and awareness to be able to do consistently whenever negative emotions rise up. If you feel something is amiss 10x a day, you can carve out 10x of these deep breathing exercises each day as well. Try it and let me know your results.

Chapter 6:

Distraction Is Robbing You

Every second you spend doing something that is not moving you
towards your goal, you are robbing yourself of precious time.
Stop being distracted!

You have something you need to do,
but for some reason become distracted by
other less important tasks and procrastinate on the important stuff.
Most people do it,
whether it's notification s on your phone or chat with colleges,
mostly less than half the working day is productive.

Distraction can be avoided by having a schedule
which should include some down time to relax
or perhaps get some of them distractions out of the way,
but time limited.

As long as everything has its correct time in
your day you can keep distraction from stealing too much of your time.
When your mind is distracted it becomes nearly impossible to
concentrate on the necessary work at hand.
Always keep this question in mind:
"is what I am about to do moving me towards my goal?"

If not, is it necessary?

What could I do instead that will?

It's all about your 24 hours.

Your actions and the reactions to your actions from that day,

good or bad.

By keeping your mind focused on your schedule that

moves you towards your goal, you will become resilient to distraction.

Distraction is anything that is not on your schedule.

You may need to alter that depending on the importance of the

intrusion.

Being successful means becoming single minded about your goal.

Those with faith do not need a plan b because they know plan A is the

only way and they refuse to accept anything else.

Any time you spend contemplating failure will add to its chances of

happening.

Why not focus on what will happen if you succeed instead?

Distraction from your vision of success is one of its biggest threats.

Blocking out distraction and keeping that vision clear is key.

Put that phone on flight mode and turn off the TV.

Focus on the truly important stuff.

If you don't do it, it will never get done.

The responsibility is all yours for everything in your life.

The responsibility is yours to block out the distractions and exercise your free-will over your thoughts and actions.

By taking responsibility and control you will become empowered.

Refuse to let anyone distract you when you're working.

Have a set time in your schedule to deal with stuff not on the schedule.

This will allow you time to deal with unexpected issues without stopping you doing the original work.

The reality is that we all only have so much time.

Do you really want to waste yours on distractions?

Do you want to not hit your target because of them?

Every time you stop for a notification on your phone you are losing time from your success.

Don't let distraction rob you of another second, minute, hour or day.

Days turn to months and months turn to years don't waste time on distractions and fears.

Chapter 7:

Things That Spark Joy

I'm sure you've heard the term "spark joy", and this is our topic of discussion today that I am going to borrow heavily from Marie Kondo.

Now why do I find the term spark joy so fascinating and why have i used it extensively in all areas of my life ever since coming across that term a few years ago?

When I first watched Marie Kondo's show on Netflix and also reading articles on how this simple concept that she has created has helped people declutter their homes by choosing the items that bring joy to them and discarding or giving away the ones that don't, I began my own process of decluttering my house of junk from clothes to props to ornaments, and even to furniture.

I realised that many things that looked good or are the most aesthetically pleasing, aren't always the most comfortable to use or wear. And when they are not my go to choice, they tend to sit on shelves collecting dust and taking up precious space in my house. And after going through my things one by one, this recurring theme kept propping up time and again. And i subconsciously associated comfort and ease of use with things that spark joy to me. If I could pick something up easily without hesitation to use or wear, they tend to me things that I gravitated to naturally, and these things began to spark joy when i used them. And when i started getting rid of things that I don't find particularly pleased to use, i felt my house was only filled with enjoyable things that I not only enjoyed looking at, but also using on a regular and frequent basis.

This association of comfort and ease of use became my life philosophy. It didn't apply to simply just decluttering my home, but also applied to the process of acquiring in the form of shopping. Every time i would pick something up and consider if it was worthy of a purpose, i would examine whether this thing would be something that I felt was comfortable and that i could see myself utilising, and if that answer was no, i would put them down and never consider them again because i knew deep down that it would not spark joy in me as I have associated joy with comfort.

This simple philosophy has helped saved me thousands of dollars in frivolous spending that was a trademark of my old self. I would buy things on the fly without much consideration and most often they would end up as white elephants in my closet or cupboard.

To me, things that spark joy can apply to work, friends, and relationships as well. Expanding on the act of decluttering put forth by Marie Kondo. If the things you do, and the people you hang out with don't spark you much joy, then why bother? You would be better off spending time doing things with people that you actually find fun and not waste everybody's time in the process. I believe you would also come out of it being a much happier person rather than forcing yourself to be around people and situations that bring you grief.

Now that is not to say that you shouldn't challenge yourself and put yourself out there. But rather it is to give you a chance to assess the things you do around you and to train yourself to do things that really spark joy in you that it becomes second nature. It is like being fine tuned to your 6th sense in a way because ultimately we all know what we truly like and dislike, however we choose to ignore these feelings and that costs us time effort and money.

So today's challenge is for you to take a look at your life, your home, your friendships, career, and your relationships. Ask yourself, does this thing spark joy? If it doesn't, maybe you should consider a decluttering of sorts from all these different areas in your life and to streamline it to a more minimalist one that you can be proud of owning each and every piece.

Take care and I'll see you in the next one.

Chapter 8:

Dealing With Uncertainty in Job Applications

Today we are going to touch on the topic of Job applications. While applying for jobs may be a daunting task, many a times, the wait for a response from any one of your applications may prove to be an even greater challenge. You see many of us live in fear that no one will take up on our offer to show them what we are capable of. It is not that we are lacking in any specific quality, but it is the fact that competition has become so fierce that it takes time and effort from the HR team to go through the hundreds of applications that may come in for any particular position.

Many times companies can take anywhere from 3-6 months or even longer to get back to you, or you may never even hear from them at all, which is also quite common. This does not mean you are unqualified or incapable, it just means a no for now.

The wait is always the hardest people we start to fill our minds with doubts. Doubts on whether we will ever be able to find another job again, doubts on whether we are worthy enough, doubts on whether we are capable enough, and worst of all, doubting our abilities and questioning our beliefs. Uncertainty can spiral into fear, and fear can consume us if we don't things more lightly.

So what do i suggest you do while you wait for a reply? Instead of sitting around and checking your email everyday for a potential response, why don't you go search up ways that you can make money on the side that does not require a full time job. The internet has become a powerful tool to make money, and it is a fair game that requires only your time and effort to create a business that is independent of any potential employer or HR department. You might find that learning a new skill to make money online can potentially become a part time career that you can pursue to generate income on the side while you wait for a favourable reply from a company.

Having done this myself, i have tried numerous times to apply to standard job roles that appear on job search sites. But i have found myself to be lacking in certain areas of experience that is required because I have spent most of my time after graduating college on trying to make money online. And these skills that I have acquired may not translate directly to any formal job because they are quite niche and specific. I have found however that embarking on a road less travelled has proved to be engaging and challenging at the same time.

And whilst I have still job applications that are awaiting a response, I no longer feel anxiety towards them and look forward to them as a bonus as I have build multiple side incomes that have allowed me not to lay all my eggs in one basket. This wide net that I have cast provides me with a greater sense of security and it has helped me to deal with the uncertainty of job applications greatly.

I challenge each and every one of you today to take some chances while u wait, and who knows, this part time side income that you have generate could one day overtake the salary that a standard job would ever be able to give you. Of course u can also take the time to apply for more jobs should you wish, but never just sit around and wait because waiting can be dangerous if you dont know how to manage your emotions well.

Take care and I wish you all the best in your job applications and careers. I'll see you in the next one.

Chapter 9:

Bounce Back From Failure

Failure is a big word. It is a negative word most say. It is cursed in most cases. It is frowned upon when it is on your plate. But why?

Sure, it certainly doesn't feel good when you encounter failure. We can't even forgive ourselves for failing at a simple card game. We get impatient, we get hopeless and ultimately we get depressed on even the smallest of failure we go through in everyday life.

Why is it that way? Why can't we try to change a failure into something better? Why can't we just leave that failure right there and not try to make a big deal out of each and every small little setback?

These questions have a very deep meaning and a very important place in everyone's life.

Let's start with the simplest step to make it easy for yourself to deal with a certain failure. Whenever you fail at anything, just pause for a second and talk to yourself.

Rewind what you just went through. Talk to yourself through the present circumstances. Think about what you could have done to improve at what you just did. Think about what you could have done to prevent whatever tragic incident you went through. Or what you could have done to do better at what you felt like failing at.

These questions will immediately sketch a scenario in front of your eyes. A scenario where you can actually see yourself flourishing and doing your best against all odds.

Whatever happened to you, I am sure you didn't deserve it. But so what if you

Lost some money or a loved one or your pet? Ask yourself this, is it the end of the world? Have you stopped breathing? Have you no reason left to keep living?

You had, you have, and you will always have a new thing, a new person a new place to start with. Life has endless possibilities for you to find. But you just have to bounce back from whatever setback you think you cannot get out of.

Take for example the biggest tech billionaires in the world. I am giving this example because people tend to relate more to these examples these days. Elon Musk started his carrier with a small office with his brother and they both lived in the same office for a whole year. They couldn't even afford a small place for themselves to rent.

There was a time when Elon had to decide to split his last set of investments between two companies. If he had invested in one, the other would have gone down for sure, just to give a chance to the other company to maybe become their one big hit. Guess what, he ended up keeping them both because he invested in both.

Why did he succeed? Was it because he wasn't afraid? No!

He succeeded because he had Faith after all the failures he had faced. He knew that if he kept trying against all odds and even the obvious risks, he will ultimately succeed at something for what he worked so hard for all this time!

Chapter 10:

When It's Okay to Do Nothing

Today I'm going to talk about the topic of when it is okay to do nothing. We're going to be really specific with this one, and that is talking about relaxation and switching off for a while if we feel like life just seems a little too stressful or hard to take.

For many of us who are leading busy lives, life can seem like one big endless to-do list. We attract problems everyday - whether it be from our jobs, our relationships, or children, our parents, our friends, our hobbies, there just doesn't seem like a time when we can just simply do nothing. We are constantly told to keep busy with our lives, to always be doing something, to always be productive, that we forget that sometimes doing nothing may be the best thing once in a while.

As life gets more complicated, so do our problems and responsibilities. From managing a family, paying our bills, being on time with our taxes, expenses, moving houses, changing jobs, we never run out of things to fill our time with. We expand our resources with time and energy day in and day out, never resting, and it takes a huge toll on our bodies physically, mentally, emotionally, and spiritually.

When we operate on such a high level every single day, sometimes even on auto-pilot due to the routine nature of things, we might end up losing sight of who we are and why we are placed on this Earth. We may start to forget why we are doing what we are doing and we simply get lost in the ocean of tasks that need to be completed.

Many of us think that travel is the best time to recharge and relax - but for many of us who plan elaborate trips, travel can sometimes be as exhausting as going to work although with a different agenda. With the limited time we have on our travel and leaves that we are allowed to take, we jam pack our schedule that requires detailed planning and execution. Rushing from place to place to check off landmarks of interests can sometimes be a chore in itself. If we are not careful, even travel can drain us the same way. So what should we do then?

How about nothing?

How about absolutely nothing.

Doing nothing might sound curious to many of you. "What do you mean do nothing?" Some of you might say. It is exactly what it says.

When we have nothing on our agenda, nothing to plan for and nothing to deal with, we find ourselves in a space of our own. A space where we can reflect on the things that are happening in our lives. A space where we can look inwards to check on our current state and feelings. To get in touch with ourselves to see the areas where we might want to improve on. And to be reminded of the direction that we are headed.

You can do nothing by simply finding a quiet place in your house or elsewhere, where you decide to give however long you need to recharge holistically. To make "doing nothing" successful, you have to set yourself up for success. Decide that you will switch off all electronic devices - to purge yourself of technology, of reminders, of deadlines, of your bosses and colleagues, and to find your inner quiet.

If you find sitting quietly and being by yourself can be too daunting of a task, consider finding a guided meditation guide or some soothing music where you can just simply lie and rest uninterrupted. If sleep is what you need in that moment, take a nap. If ideas flash before you, acknowledge them, write them down, your call. Listen to your body and respond to it.

When you practice doing nothing consistently, you will feel that life starts to slow down a little bit more. You start to breathe a little slower and life becomes slightly more manageable when you learn how to take care of yourself.

Instead of only looking forward to holidays and trips to recharge, learn to schedule doing nothing routinely in your calender. Having the ability and power to choose as and when you need to relax and give full and total attention to yourself is as important as the attention and time you give to those around you. Only when you can take care of yourself first can you also take care of others with the same capacity.

So I challenge each and every one of you to put yourself first by making the decision to do nothing. That it is perfectly okay to switch off the crazy life around you for a moment. You can always come back to it once you're fully recharged and ready to rumble again.

Being Mentally Strong

Have you ever wondered why your performance in practice versus an actual test is like night and day? Or how you are able to perform so well in a mock situation but just crumble when it comes game time?

It all boils down to our mental strength.

The greatest players in sports all have one thing in common, incredibly strong beliefs in themselves that they can win no matter how difficult the circumstance. Where rivals that have the same playing ability may challenge them, they will always prevail because they know their self-worth and they never once doubt that they will lose even when facing immense external or internal pressure.

Most of us are used to facing pressure from external sources. Whether it be from people around us, online haters, or whoever they may be, that can take a toll on our ability to perform. But the greatest threat is not from those areas... it is from within. The voices in our head telling us that we are not going to win this match, that we are not going to well in this performance, that we should just give up because we are already losing by that much.

It is only when we can crush these voices that we can truly outperform our wildest abilities. Mental strength is something that we can all acquire. We just have to find a way to block out all the negativity and replace them with voices that are encouraging. to believe in ourselves that we can and will overcome any situation that life throws at us.

The next time you notice that doubts start creeping in, you need to snap yourself out of it as quickly as you can, 5 4 3 2 1. Focus on the next point, focus on the next game, focus on the next speech. Don't give yourself the time to think about what went wrong the last time. You are only as good as your present performance, not your past.

I believe that you will achieve wonderful things in life you are able to crush those negative thoughts and enhance your mental strength.

CPSIA information can be obtained
at www.ICGtesting.com
Printed in the USA
LVHW081507241221
707138LV00022B/2527